How to Write an Effective Marketing Plan

A guide for SMEs that want more marketing
success

L.D. Woodward

For further information please visit
www.l-w-marketing.com.

CONTENTS

Introduction

There is only one place to start. That is to answer the key question: what is marketing? If you're going to get success from it, then you definitely need to understand it. Whenever I tell people I work in marketing, the first question that usually pops out of their mouths is, "So you do social media?" But actually, when you think about the reality of what marketing is, this is like saying to a Decathlete, so you do a bit of running?

My favourite definition of marketing comes from the Chartered Institute of Marketing (well, you would hope they'd get it right!). It says: "Marketing is the management process responsible for identifying, anticipating and satisfying customer requirements profitably."

When people assume marketing is activities like social media, they're getting mixed up with marketing tactics. That's just one element of marketing. It isn't really what marketing is all about. It's actually all about your customers. Without customers, you haven't got a business. So you need to put them at the heart of everything you do.

Never make any decisions because you like the idea of it. Make decisions because you know it will work for your customers, be it current ones or prospective.

In this guide, we're going to be working through how to produce an effective marketing plan, and it's really aimed at small to medium businesses. There are hundreds of additional things that you could do on top of the recommendations that I detail. But I've been working in marketing for a long time, and I've always worked for Small to Medium Enterprises (SME). Therefore I've used all my experience and training to strip everything back, and I've come up with a method that is simple and useful. It won't take loads of time to develop, but it will help you focus your efforts and attune your marketing to both your business and your customers.

As you work through this guide, you will find a lot of suggestions of things that you could do. That doesn't mean I'm recommending that you should do them all. There is no template for marketing, so I've discussed a lot of different ideas in order to cover a lot of different industries and company types. The only thing that is important for you, though, is what will work for your business. Nothing else matters.

One of the things that I learnt early on in marketing is that it's just as important to realise the tasks that you shouldn't be doing, as it is to home in on the tasks that you know will work. Not everyone is naturally a planner, but one of the reasons that a marketing plan works so well is that it helps you decide exactly what activities to execute and what to omit with confidence. Trying a bit of everything is such a waste of time. Time that most businesses just don't have. Ultimately you can spend ages doing something that would never work. This plan will help you pinpoint exactly what should and shouldn't work, meaning you'll put your time, effort and budget to where it's going to be most effective.

The other benefit to planning is that you'll become better perceived by your audience. A scattergun approach isn't just a poor use of time and money, but it sends the message out to your audience that you're all over the place. A well thought through, consistent and persistent approach says you're in control, professional and can be trusted. Just sending out that message alone is hugely powerful. But you simply can't do that without a marketing plan.

Putting together the ideas in this guide won't cost you anything but a bit of time, but it could seriously improve your marketing. That being the case, I strongly urge you to give it a go. You have very little to lose and masses to gain. Best of luck!

Marketing Solves Problems

If you're going to write a marketing plan that is going to have any chance of being effective, then you need to give it an ultimate purpose. It's no good just saying I want to market my business. All you'll end up doing are some arbitrary tasks that won't lead anywhere or have any real purpose.

My mantra is "be purpose driven". If you give everything a purpose then you'll never end up doing anything just for the sake of it and everything will have a good chance of success. And you'll be able to measure that success because you'll know whether it achieved what you wanted it to achieve in the first place. It's a full circle of ticks.

For your marketing plan, I recommend that the purpose should be thought of as a problem you want to solve. If you think of it like that, you'll have a thread running through your work. You'll identify a problem you want to solve, so you'll work through the steps of exactly how to solve it, and then you'll put yourself in the best possible position to end up with a positive result.

You could also call it an objective, but I think problem solving gets your brain in the right gear. It becomes a challenge that you can actually achieve rather than a goal in the future you hope to reach.

It's ultimately the same thing, but I think solving a business problem is more motivational. It's stating what you want to achieve so you can work out how actually to achieve it.

Research suggests that identifying two or three problems/objectives is probably a good thing, but the more objectives you have, the more detailed your plan is going to need to be. So if this is your first time developing a marketing plan, I would recommend starting off easy and just picking one problem or objective to work to.

Choosing the Problem

During this book I'm going to work through a case study to help bring to life what I'm trying to explain. It's a real life plan that I worked on and we achieved amazing results. But to protect who it is, let's just call it "Company Q".

I was hired by the company to look after all its marketing. But that's a huge thing to consider. That could cover anything and everything. So the first place to start was to identify what issues there were and, more specifically, what the company wanted to achieve. That helped me simplify my thoughts and give the marketing some direction.

The main problem that Company Q faced was that, to all intents and purposes, it was starting from scratch. Despite the fact that the company was a few years old, the directors had never hired a marketing professional before to do the marketing. Any efforts at marketing previous to this had been ad hoc at best. Work had come in from the sales team's contacts, but the company now wanted to grow and it had big growth targets. It was time for them to get moving and they knew this.

So the key objectives were:

1. Get the name Company Q known in the market
2. Generate leads to help the company reach its ambitious growth target

That was it. Everything else was secondary. The plan was ultimately going to come down to brand awareness and lead generation. From the second you've thought about your rationale, you have a focus. Nothing else matters. You're already tuned in. The most important thing now is not to forget that. Everything you do in the plan must come back to the objectives, whether you have one or four.

I've described what was needed for Company Q, but there are dozens of other problems you might want to solve. Do you identify with any of these?

- If I lost one client, I wouldn't be able to pay the bills, so I need more clients
- A new competitor has just launched and is stealing my market share
- I only get business through word of mouth, so I need to expand how people find out about me if I want to grow
- We've just launched this amazing new product, but no one is buying it
- Our brand looks tired and old. We need a face lift and we need it to resonate better with our customers
- The current economic state is having a huge impact on my business and I need to find a way to counteract it

These are just examples. It literally could be

anything. Think about your business and what you want to achieve. There is no off the shelf marketing plan that will work. It has to be about your individual circumstances. If you try something someone else has done, you're not giving yourself the best chance of success. Developing a plan finely tuned to your business will give you the best possible outcome. Why would you settle for anything less?

Marketing Audit

A Marketing Audit is quite simply as it sounds: it audits everything relating to your market and your marketing, letting you see what has been happening, what is happening and what will affect your business.

Do Your Research

You can tell the difference between someone who understands marketing and someone who doesn't. This is a very important point. Someone untrained will plough straight into the actions. And it will most likely have a strong digital focus. That's because digital is widely accessible, easy to execute and easy to monitor. But the second you start to do any training in marketing, you realise how terrible that approach is. Not only because it completely overlooks the full marketing mix, but also because jumping straight into the actions without asking any of the key questions first will mean your actions have absolutely no foundation.

Anyone who understands marketing will tell you the only place to start is to do research. We call it a Marketing Audit. How could you ever expect to produce anything of quality if you don't fully understand all the factors involved? It's just common sense.

If you were buying a car, it's highly unlikely that you'd just buy the first one you saw. You might do some research, see what other people are driving, go for a test drive and make sure you're getting the best value for money. If you want to have the best car for you, then you take the time to think about it properly. So why when you're investing time and money in marketing would you just jump straight in by posting lots of stuff on social media? Without prior consideration, you might end up with a car that is vastly overpriced and riddled with problems, and it works the same in marketing. You may end up doing activities that are actually detrimental to your brand or counterproductive to what you actually want to achieve. It's so easy to get it wrong. I see it all the time.

Often when I suggest to people that we should conduct a Marketing Audit before doing anything else, they immediately tell me they know their market. They know their customers. They've been doing it for a long time and they know what it's all about.

But I always ask: in the time that they've been doing it, how has the world changed? In just six months, so much can happen. I do a lot of training on marketing, and I'm blown away by how quickly I can get behind if I don't stay on top of things. Especially in the digital arena. Things massively move forward every few months at least. The world is changing fast, and this is relevant in practically every industry. If you want to stay ahead of the game, you need to keep tabs on what's going on out there.

Even if you believe you are on top of everything, still don't skip this step. I'm yet to do a Marketing

Audit for anyone who hasn't been surprised by at least some of the data or information found. If nothing else, it forces you to take a good look at the decisions you've made, giving you the chance to evaluate if everything is still working as you'd expect it to. You simply can't lose by taking the time to do the research.

Also, never ever use gut instinct. There's a time and a place for instinct, and the planning phase isn't it. It has to be built on absolute fact, and going by your gut doesn't guarantee anything. You run the risk of creating a biased plan and that makes the whole project a waste of time.

Finding the Time

One of the key problems when working for a small company is that time becomes stretched. It's inevitable that fewer people will have to do more of the work. You're likely to have one person doing multiple different roles, and every day is a battle to do the work that pays the bills. And that payable work has to take priority. So it's a fair question to ask if you think: "How on earth am I going to find the time to do research?"

When it comes to a Marketing Audit, research is quite an open word. It could mean lots of different things. A large company may spend six months extensively researching a broad range of elements, drilling down into minute detail so that they can gain a real competitive edge. They could study all different stakeholders, do in-depth analysis on sales stats, break down the full customer journey and evaluate each aspect of it. Under any rock, they could find the answer that will give them the upper hand and help them reach their customers in a more engaging way.

But a large company may also have a team dedicated just to that very job. A Strategic Marketing Manager is there to work on the Marketing Plan. That's their focus; full time. Then there's a whole other team there to execute it. It's much easier when you have nothing else to do.

On the flipside, if you're an SME, you simply won't have the resource to spend ages on the research element. You have a million other things to do, and you're probably already working eighteen hours a day.

But actually, that might be for the best. Spending ages on research will probably be an unwise use of your time anyway. Fundamentally, the more research you do, the more you'll understand, yes. But when you think about it, what are you going to do with all that understanding? You could fine tune your marketing plan, develop an award-winning campaign and steal all the marketing share from your competitors. With that much knowledge, you'll be in a strong position to achieve anything. However, if you suddenly got thousands of leads in, would you be able to deal with them? If you weren't able to respond to all the leads you generated, your campaign would unravel quicker than you could say audit.

One of the most important aspects for any business plan is to be realistic, and you have to be realistic across every aspect of what you're doing. Therefore you need to put the work in to give you the results you want. You don't need to do any more. Not at the moment.

For Company Q, I spent about a week properly pulling together research, sitting with different departments and analysing data. They wanted to reach a turnover that was in the millions not thousands, and we needed hundreds of leads to make that possible. Therefore I planned to do enough research to give me a decent level of information that would enable us to reach that goal.

A sole trader, with perhaps a more modest objective in mind, might only need to spend a day doing research at the most. One day of proper thinking could change the outcome of annual results. If you think about the return on investment, it's worth one day. Sure, you won't be able to pull together reams of information that will blow your customers away and leave your competition eating your dust. But is that what you want anyway? You can do that in year four when you've grown a bit more and you have more staff to support you. Being realistic is a key part of being purpose driven.

The one week of solid research I did for Company Q was definitely time well spent. I could have just jumped right in. Tried a bit of blogging, a bit of social media, some PR and advertising, maybe have put on a few events. We might have got some leads.

But, as you'll see as your plan develops, without an idea running through all your activity, and without it actually working directly towards a specific goal, it just becomes meaningless humdrum. Of course, a few people may react. Perhaps those who want something in return. Perhaps people you already know. Reaching people who have no clue you even exist at the moment is a whole other game, and that takes time, effort and understanding. To get the best results you simply can't cheat the system.

Therefore, decide what you want to achieve and be honest about how big those goals are, and then put aside what you believe to be a fair amount of time. Believe me, when you start doing research, you can get sucked into it. You could be looking forever. So plan your time carefully and think about your return on investment. Whatever you put in, you need to make sure it balances with what you want out of it.

What to Look at

I have recommended four key areas to focus your research on. There are hundreds of other things you could look at, but to optimise your time and to get the information that will give you a good holistic view of your market and company, I recommend doing just these things. They're core elements that I've always found to be incredibly powerful. Hopefully you might find a few surprises.

1. Industry Research

The first area to look at is what's going on outside of your company. In marketing we call this the Macro Environment. It's anything external to your company that you have no control over but could affect your business.

A PESTEL is my favourite way of analysing the Macro Environment. It lists seven areas that cover such a wide variety of things. If you're not familiar with a PESTEL, then it looks at the following factors:

- Political
- Economical
- Social

- Technological
- Environmental
- Legal

For each element you need to list all the areas that can or will affect your business. I then like to state whether each area is a threat or opportunity, to help highlight it. Finally, I'll make a statement about what that means to the business. For example, if a new standard was coming into play but it wasn't mandatory, I might say it was an opportunity. I would then comment on what the pros and cons were of meeting this standard. You only need a short note that you can reflect upon after the other parts of the audit are completed.

You don't have to go into that level of detail, but I find it helps if I jot down bits of evaluation along the way.

Let's take a look in more depth.

Political

Political looks at all the government related factors, such as policies and regulations, or government targets. What official elements are there that you need to abide by? What could perhaps affect your business or, just as importantly, will affect your customers?

If all your customers have to have a product to meet a certain regulation and you just happen to sell that product, that's a huge opportunity. It's a simple example, but here you have to explore all factors. It may be that there are policies that you don't have to legally abide by, but those who do will gain a competitive advantage. Is this something to consider?

I encourage you here not just to write down what you think you know, but actually take a few minutes to find out if there's anything you've missed. For every industry, there are official sites with objective information. Take a look and see what you can find. There might be something in there that could be a huge advantage to your business.

If you do want to add in a little more detail, for everything you list - perhaps as a bullet point - state whether it's a threat or opportunity to your business and put a note of what action, if any, needs to be taken. You aren't making decisions on your plan here, you're just noting anything worth considering so it's easy for you to scan through later.

Economical

What economic factors can or will affect your business? This is vital if you import and export, but, even if you just sell nationally, the economy is still a large area to consider. You need to think about your supply chain and your customers. Are your customers generally tightening their purse strings due to current economic factors, or do you focus on those who have a bit more disposable income?

Do seasons affect your business? Are you always going to be busier at Christmas, and, if so, what predictions are there for this year? What is actually happening out there?

You don't have to be au fait with The Financial Times to complete this section usefully, but taking some time to look into both how your business operates and what is happening with your customers in relation to the economy could make a big impact on how you decide to plan your marketing activities.

Social

This is more about society and how we work. For example, what are the culture and beliefs of your customers and how is that going to affect what you do? It doesn't have to be religious. It could relate to ethics, sustainability or tradition. Then what are the typical behaviours that you need to understand? Are there any trends or habits worth tuning into?

How customers interact with media is a good example. Are your customers all focused online? If so, what platforms do they tend to use? How do they spend their day? Has there been a recent kickback and they're turning off social media and wanting more offline ways to receive their information? Or are they all obsessed with Snapchat?

There is so much free research available that analyses cultural trends. But this isn't about studying people in general. Consider your market and focus on that. What one group of people does is very different to another. Age, gender, social status, occupation - they're all contributing factors. So keep in mind what's relevant for you and your business only.

Technological

This section focuses very much on how technology will impact your business. It could relate to how your company uses technology as well as how your customers interact with it. Think about how it affects both what they buy from you and how they buy from you. There will probably be a lot to consider in our modern world, and I'd suggest forgetting about the past and looking more into the future. What is around the corner? What are the big technology companies working on? What could you tap into that could boost your business? Would an App help you sell more? What about e-commerce? Think about software as well as hardware. Think about it all and take a few minutes to see what news is out there that could help.

Environmental

This is very important in today's world. It covers both what official environmental factors you need to be aware of, such as ISO 14001 or the CRC Energy Efficiency Scheme, as well as how your customers view environmental factors.

Are there things you need to comply with? What do you do with your recycling? How wasteful is your company? Could it impact how your customers perceive you? How concerned are your customers about the environment? Are they more likely to worry about your green credentials or wonder what price things will cost them? Do you even know?

If you're not sure about any of these things, that's just as valuable information. You may decide it's worth knowing and then you can add into your plan to find out that information, by sending out a survey for example. Every element of your research is important. Whether you find out things or you realise you lack knowledge, write it down.

Legal

Every company must know what legislation it needs to comply with. Whether it's GDPR, Health & Safety, Risk Assessments or consumer rights, make sure you fully understand all the legal implications in relation to what you do. If there's anything you could have overlooked, now is the time to find it out. And if there's anything that you feel is more important and you could make your customers more aware of, this is the perfect time to highlight it.

Summary

This whole exercise is not just about lifting facts for the sake of it. It's about exploring a range of external factors and then deciding how or if they can harm or benefit your business. Once you know this you can then plan effectively either to react to the potential threats or leverage the potential gains. This opens up more opportunities than there seems at first, and it's a very worthwhile exercise for a whole raft of reasons. At the very least I'd recommend you finding a couple of points in each area. You don't have to spend ages finding out every fine detail of the law, but feel confident that you've got a good grasp of things and make sure there's something useful in each section that you can take with you to the next step. That is, don't list a meaningless fact, such as "My customers spend money". Find out how, why and when they spend money. That's a wildly simple example, but I hope you see the point. The more you can make it meaningful, the more you'll get out of it.

I say it a lot. You'll get used to it: be purpose driven.

2. Customer Analysis

The next step is to analyse your customers. Here is where I see a lot of people make a key mistake. They automatically start to focus on who they believe to be their ideal customer; immediately homing in on that one type of person or business that they believe is best suited to their product or service.

However, this way of thinking can actually hinder your profits, not help them. As soon as you start focusing on one particular thing, you become blinkered to everything else. You'll focus on what you believe to be your ideal client, without truly having analysed all the possibilities. Put quite simply: without exploring every option, how could you ever know that you've made the right decision?

So rather than think "who is my ideal client", instead list out every single type of person or business that you could sell to and then make notes on them.

Let's take a look at the toy market as an example. I think this market showcases the issues quite well. If I were to ask a toy shop owner, "Who is your ideal customer?" they might say children. But actually there's a whole complex raft of things to explore if you're going to truly maximise sales.

If we were to list out every single possible type of person that might buy from or have an interest in a toy shop, the list would actually look like this:

- Babies / Toddlers
- 5-12 Year Olds
- Teenagers
- Parents
- Adult Enthusiasts
- Adults no kids
- Grandparents
- Retired Adults

We all have different needs and respond to marketing in a different way. Therefore you need to group people together in a way that makes sense, whatever the demographic. For each group you put together we call it a marketing segment.

Once you've done that, the next step is to analyse each segment, breaking down how important they are to you as a business. What purchasing power do they have? How strong is their influence? How important are they to your competitors? How profitable could they be, or would they be tough to sell to?

If we start to break the list for the toy shop down, we could begin by noting that children have no money of their own. Even if they have pocket money, it's still ultimately the parents in charge. Therefore they have very little direct purchasing power. Does that mean they aren't really customers? Of course they are. But a child's power is influence. When it comes to toys, we have to consider pester power. If the children don't ask for it, will the parents buy it?

Then there's another layer of complexity to consider. Even if the child wants it and nags their parents for it, if you haven't worked on your brand and the parents don't trust in your company, that could still have a negative impact.

Moving on, what about grandparents? How often do they buy for their grandchildren and are they easier to persuade than parents? Then what about adult enthusiasts? For some toymakers, such as Lego or Hornby, there are some adults who like the products just as much as kids.

The second you start to think about it, you'll find there are so many sets of people that you could market to. People that you may have otherwise overlooked.

If you focus in straight away and make snap

decisions, you'll probably have some sales. But if you take some time to explore all your options and think about how to segment your marketing, you'll never be in a position where you've missed an important opportunity.

Influencers

One of the most important elements that you lose when you don't explore all your options is that you never consider influencers. "Who is my ideal client?" is always a question that focuses on the buyers. But the people who can influence your sales can be just as useful to you. You might immediately think of celebrities here, but there could be much simpler ways to harness the power of influence.

As shown in the toy shop example, pester power can be a strong tool to leverage. This can work for Business-to-Business (B2B) marketing as well. If you want Business X to buy your products, then it might help if their customers were demanding it. It's an extra layer of complexity that doesn't always work, but done right it can make a massive impact.

So when analysing your customers, take a few minutes to list down every type of customer you could sell to. Be imaginative and cover all bases. It might open up a new stream to your marketing that you've never considered before.

Before I started working for Company Q, there had been a business decision to focus more heavily on the influencer market. However, there had been no solid rationale for this. The decision had been made because there hadn't been much success in what the company had been doing, so it was about trying something different. This is often a trap that a business falls into. What you actually need to do is find out things sure, and clearly evaluate what the best way forward should be. So for Company Q, as part of the audit, I listed down every single business type that we could sell to, and I rated them in relation to how useful they were going to be to meet the overall objectives.

There were so many avenues, I actually found it easier to create a market map.

If you think visually, something like the following diagram might help you. It's simple to put together. You just need to decide which products different business types/groups of people (purchasers) would buy, and then who could or would influence the purchasers to encourage the sale.

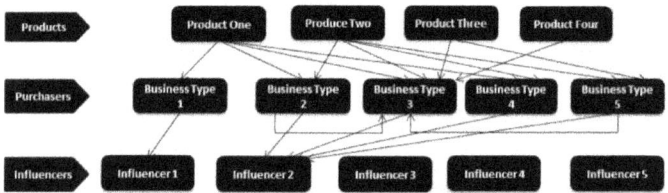

This was the type of diagram I pulled together for Company Q. It showed that there was really only one influencer that could have made a difference, and there were certain business types that could buy far more products than others. During the research phase, it's not about making decisions. It's about pulling together all the facts to help you make the right, informed decisions when you have that holistic view. A diagram like this gave me a wealth of information that I could see quite clearly, and it suggested that focusing on an influencer might not be the most profitable stream.

3. Competitor Analysis

If you want to have any real chance of producing a marketing plan that will work for you, then you can't just look at your business in isolation. You have to analyse your competitors. Positioning your company in the right way is vital, so you need to be able to identify how you can differentiate, and you can only achieve that by understanding what your competitors are doing.

Don't worry if you don't fully understand what positioning is at the minute. We'll come back to that later. All you need to do for now is make sure you're aware of what your competitors are selling and how they're marketing themselves.

Here I would suggest looking at four or five competitors. You may have dozens, and you may want to evaluate more, but think about how much time is worth dedicating to this task. If you have a lot of minor competitors and very few major ones, maybe just research all the major ones and one or two minor ones, to give you a fair variety. It's about generally understanding what is going on out there. That's all you need to achieve in this task.

What you analyse is really up to you. Before you even look at a competitor, I'd begin by deciding what you want to review, and then look at all the same things for each competitor. What you decide to review may differ depending on your industry. Some suggestions could be:

- Key products/services
- Main marketing message(s)
- Social media platforms and how often they post/what content they post
- Do they have a blog? Type of content

published
- Website set up (e-commerce? Live Chat? Downloadable content?)
- Strengths/weaknesses
- Size/turnover
- Positioning/how they differentiate themselves

You may have noticed that I haven't mentioned Unique Selling Points (USP). Listing down your competitors' USPs might have been something you would have considered. However, what I've listed instead is "how they differentiate themselves".

In a world of such great competition, it's very hard for any business to find USPs nowadays. And even if you can find something unique to your business, the very act of finding this unique feature can be quite superficial. Instead, in modern day marketing, we talk about differentiation. This is because being different and standing out runs deeper and is more emotional than a traditional list of USPs.

Every business has a story. Every brand has a reason for being there and has its own individual way of dealing with customers. This is what you need to focus on, and in this task you need to understand how your competitors are differentiating themselves. What is their story and what are their values? How are they trying to stand out in a busy market and what are they doing that's different? If anything? Once you understand this, you'll then be able to better understand how you're different and what makes you special to your customers.

But only list things about your competitors for now. We're not ready yet to make decisions about our own business. We still don't have the full holistic view.

The list of areas to review that I made are just possibilities. If there are certain things that are relevant to your industry, or you'd be very keen to find out how you compare, then include that in your own list. Once you know what you want to analyse, then start your research on each competitor. But always look for the same things and compare equally.

For Company Q, I'd been told on day one that it was the only company in the market that offered bespoke products, whereas all the competitors provided off the shelf products. The off the shelf products might have had shorter lead times as they were from stock, but they didn't suit all applications, and compromises often had to be made. Therefore Company Q could offer something far better.

The point of the Marketing Audit is to find out the facts, so I took what I'd been told and I reviewed how many products each competitor sold, what type of products, what type of businesses they worked with and how different their offering really was. I also reviewed their brands, key marketing messages and general marketing activity. I didn't take anyone's word for it, I did the research myself so I could prove it. Competitors introduce new products all the time, so it's always vital to be fully up to speed.

I found out that Company Q really was different and did stand out in the market. No other competitor could do what Company Q did, yet all of the competitors had much stronger brands, were bigger companies and were much better known. Even with a unique product offering, there was still a mountain to climb.

I was once told, "A good product sells itself." It was by someone who was arguing that more time and budget should be spent in research and development than in marketing and sales. Whilst good products that have been well thought through and manufactured to a high quality certainly do make the marketing task easier, the best product in the world won't sell if no one knows about it. And telling someone something once won't make a difference either. We need to see things about seven times before they sink in; before they really register with us. And that's then just acknowledging something's existence. There's a whole funnel to go through before someone actually buys something from you. Unless it's a low cost consumer goods product, like a chocolate bar, we don't tend to take a punt on things. We do our research, both on the product or service we're interested in and the company that is selling it. Even more so in our digital world where tangible things are harder to come by. We need to trust what we're purchasing, and businesses can't build that relationship with customers easily. It takes time and effort.

So Company Q might have had an excellent offering that I could market, but there was a long way to go before we were going to see the sales the company deserved. We had to combat well known competitors that had a loyal customer base. There is simply no way to cheat this. You need to put the work in and do things properly if you want results, and the first step is to know where you stand. Analysing your competitors gives you just that.

4. Internal Review

When you've properly examined the outside world - all those things out of your control –the final step is to honestly evaluate your business internally. This still isn't the time for making decisions. This is the time for examining everything you have been doing so that you can make sound decisions on what you need to be doing moving forward. Learning lessons from what's gone before – be it positive or negative – is one of the strongest tools we have. Marketing is a task of constant improvement. Do more of what works and avoid the things that don't. There are no guarantees of success whatever we do, but the more informed the decisions are that we make, the better the results are likely to be.

For your internal review, I recommend using the 4Ps concept.

It's been 60 years since Jerome McCarthy first proposed the 4Ps as a marketing concept. Despite all that time and all the changes in the world, they're still an important part of any marketing plan today. There is a lesson in itself that we can learn from that. Marketing fads come and go, but the core of marketing principles always stay constant. Therefore don't get swept up in what the latest cool new trend is. If you want to have the best chance of marketing success, stick to the methods that have been well considered and will help you build that solid foundation. There's a reason why some of the more traditional marketing concepts are still around today. It's because they work.

The 4Ps

I believe the 4Ps work because any marketing plan needs a firm foundation. You need to have a grasp of the key components of your business, your products and your services before you are able to make any sound decisions on marketing. The 4Ps help to give you that in such a simple way. Simple and effective. What's not to like?

Unless you're a start up business, in all of the areas of the 4Ps, you need to look at what you have done previously. It's about analysing the past to help shape the future. I'd recommend going back over about 3 years of data, if you can. Even if you've been trading for longer, just stick to 3 years. That will provide enough data to give you a good understanding. If you've been trading for less than 3 years, just do what you can. And if you're a start up, add in all your plans to date, or write down what decisions you need to make, so you can get a full view of all that you want to do so you can properly evaluate how and if it will work.

Let's breakdown the 4Ps:

Product

In this first area, you need to take a look at your range of products, or services if that's what you do. I would advise you to list everything you sell or offer. Although, if you have a catalogue of products, it's probably not wise to list every single item. Perhaps just list each range. You need to cover everything, but not drown in too much information either.

First of all create a list and then comment upon each area. As I said before, this isn't about making decisions, it's about reflecting on what has been done.

It may be useful to detail the distinctions between the different parts of your offering. Is it clear? Have things become blended over time? Would you say it's a simple offering that you can effectively communicate or could there be a danger of overwhelming your audience?

The next step is to look at value. This is one of the most important yet often overlooked areas for any business. People don't buy things because you tell them to (not generally). People buy because, in some way, they get something out of it. We always buy things for our own reasons. It's because the product or service will benefit us or be useful to us in some way. Therefore, the more you can focus on the value you offer to clients, the more success you'll have. You'll cut through all the waffle and get straight to the point of what your customers need to know. So in your Product list, perhaps make a note of how each of your products (or range of products) or services actually helps your customers. Why are your customers going to buy it or buy into it?

I always find it useful to ask, "So what?" If your product descriptions are simply a list of components or a list of banal features and benefits, your customers may very well unconsciously ask, "So what?" Why should they care? You need to make sure that anything you say about your products and services gives your customers the right information and will encourage them to buy.

Let's look at an example. Going back to our fake toy shop, let's pretend we're promoting a brand new board game. This is an exaggerated example, but hopefully you'll see the point.

This is the very basic marketing that some people use:

"Our new board game is easy to play for up to 8 people aged 4 upwards. We have designed it so it can be played anywhere and is good for travelling. It is robust and the parts won't easily break, meaning it will last a long time. It is ideal to play with the family at Christmas. This board game is very popular and stocks are limited."

So what?

Now, let's think about why people play board games and bring out the value:

"Brighten up those boring family dinners with our brand new board game. Up to 8 people can play from aged 4 upwards, meaning no one has to miss out. It really is great fun for everyone. With a compact design, it's also perfect for taking away on holiday. Why not bring that competitive edge to sunny evenings? Available now. But be quick, this hugely popular board game is selling fast. Want to see what all the fuss is about?"

People don't buy board games because they like the idea of it. They buy them as entertainment. They buy them to give the family something to do that's sociable and enjoyable. Whatever you sell, think about why people would buy from you – what they get out of it - and make sure you properly tap into that in your marketing.

Moving on within the Product area, you may also want to think about the lifecycle of the product or service. If it lasts forever, you might be unlikely to have repeat business, but if it's not well made, will your customers come back to buy again?

Then what are the pros and cons of each product or service? Everything has a strength and weakness. Make sure you've fully considered them across all of your offering.

You don't need to comment on everything. Pick what you think is important. This task is about writing down a range of facts to give you a holistic picture of your offering. You don't need to drill down into the minute detail. You just need enough data to give you that picture. Perhaps a picture you might not have appreciated before.

One further step here that I'd recommend is to properly analyse your sales. Don't guess what your best seller is, actually go into your database and take a look. This may highlight product lines that really aren't working or services that no one actually wants. It will also highlight the products that really are selling well. If you aren't able to pull up sales data, that in itself is telling. Perhaps you need to review your systems.

There is no negative in taking a look at what's going on. No matter what the outcome, it's about being honest and deciding what you can do to improve things.

Price

The next area to review is your pricing. This isn't just about how much you charge, it's also about the value you offer customers and how you fit into the market.

Firstly, state your pricing structure and then evaluate both how you came to make that decision and how that fits in with your competitors. Are you cheap, in the middle ground or expensive?

It's also a very good idea to reflect upon perception. Whenever we pay for anything, we automatically assess the value of the price. Do we feel we're getting a bargain, or do we feel we're being ripped off? Whatever end of the scale you look at, there are negative and positive connotations.

For starters, whilst we all love a bargain, we're also wary of things that are too cheap. Cheap is often associated with poor quality. Therefore, even if you can afford to do things at a cheaper price, sometimes inflating your costs slightly could increase sales because people will see it as better quality.

But at the same time, if you put your costs up too much you can price yourself out of the market. If people don't believe they're getting a return on investment then they may be put off, even if they could afford the higher price. So alongside thinking about what you're charging, think about how your prices come across to your audience. Perception in marketing is everything.

It may be that you've never thought too much about your prices. If that's the case then this is the opportunity for you to explore the reasons behind that. Have you just been plucking prices out of the air? Have you been copying the competition? If you've not put much thought into it before, one of the activities you could add into your marketing plan is to do some pricing research and find out what works and what doesn't for your customers. But all you need to do is make notes at this stage and highlight areas for further consideration. Until you've examined everything, you shouldn't make any firm decisions.

For Company Q, I found that we were quite highly priced, but as we sold more bespoke items there was a perceived value to what we offered. People could pay cheaper to get something that was almost right, or pay a little bit more for Company Q to meet exact specifications. From a marketing perspective, it was an easy sell. I just needed to make sure that the rest of the brand supported the perception of high quality that the product and pricing decisions conveyed.

If the brand looked poor, no one would believe that it would be worth paying more. If people were going to believe that Company Q could offer the quality of products that they could, the brand image needed to reflect that. It's vital to have a consistent approach through all of your marketing if you want people to properly buy into what you do and the value they will get from you - whether it's cheap and cheerful and gets the job done, or more costly but higher quality.

Just as the Company Q case study shows, when you've established your pricing and where you fit into the market, you need to make sure that your brand supports that. It doesn't matter what the level of skill you have, how much experience or expertise, or how good your products really are, if your prices are at the top end and you then send a brochure to a client that's clearly been made in Word, the two aspects don't fit together. If you want people to pay a premium price, you need to ooze quality throughout. That doesn't mean to say if you're cheap, it's all right to have poor quality marketing materials, but the expectation from customers won't be the same.

So think about your prices and then think about the overall perception that your brand emits.

Place

Alongside what you sell and how much you sell it for, where you sell is just as important. This is where we start to consider the customer journey. You could have the best product with the most desired pricing, but if there are barriers in the selling process, it will all fall down.

Here you need to detail where you sell – and list all the channels. For example, do you sell online or do you have a shop? Do you have both? If you have more than one way that customers can buy from you, which way works best? Are there any barriers that might be hindering one way of selling? For example, if you sell online, is your website easy to use and does the e-commerce work effectively?

You should also evaluate any third parties here, like resellers or distributors. How effective are those channels? Is it something that could be expanded on or would it be more beneficial to bring things in house?

The only right answer is what is going to work best for your business and your customers. The easier you can make the sales journey, the better.

When we talk about the customer journey, it's about what happens from the moment the customer first hears about your products or services, all the way to them actually successfully purchasing. Have you ever plotted what that might look like and how easy it is for customers to navigate? Are you limiting yourself by not being in many places therefore customers have little chance of hearing about what you have to offer? Now is the time to think about it all. It may be that you need to change nothing, but by properly exploring all the options and considering what else could be done, you'll know the decisions you do ultimately make will be the right ones.

For Company Q, they sold some products directly through the in house sales team and others through third party distributors. The first thing I did was find out which channel here was more effective.

Looking at the sales data that I'd sourced for the Product part of the 4Ps, I found that the direct selling brought in vastly more income overall, but the trends were also unreliable and varied. There could be some very productive months that brought in vast amounts of income, and then other months that had very little. So whereas overall it seemed like a much better source of income for the company, it was also unstable. It really was down to when the customers planned their own work in, and Company Q couldn't influence it at all. We just had to be there as and when customers might want to use the products; which literally could be any time of the year. It was completely unpredictable.

On the other side, the products sold through the distributors, while vastly cheaper and providing far less overall income, did provide regular steady income that could be far more relied upon. The business couldn't have survived on these sales alone, but it was a constant stream that could help when the larger products weren't being sold. The marketing plan had to make sure that it supported both channels here. They were both needed.

The next step was to evaluate how leads came into the business. I found that the website and the telephone system were the two main sources for leads, however no logging of leads had ever been done. Emails or phone calls came in and were passed on accordingly, but it was impossible to tell how many were potential sales, who dealt with them, what they were for and whether they converted. I highlighted that there was a gap here and setting up a reporting system might be a good task for the marketing plan.

Now we're working through the 4Ps, you can see how the different areas all overlap. You really do need that holistic view before you can make any reasonable decisions.

Promotion

Finally, we have promotion. This is the area that everyone considers when it comes to marketing, but the 4Ps prove it's only one part of the mix.

This section is about looking at how you've been promoting your business to date and, more importantly, what the results of that promotion have been. This isn't about reviewing what you have planned in. This is detailing the work you've already done.

Whenever I work with businesses on this area, I ask them to list every type of promotional activity they'd tried, whether it worked or not. So that's all campaigns, social media activity, adverts, events, PR and so on. It's also the perfect time to look at your Google Analytics to see what's been happening on your website.

Furthermore, explore your database and other marketing systems you use, if relevant. How effective have they been? Are there training issues or funding issues that are holding you or your team back? What has the return on investment been and how have things ended up compared to your plans?

It's important to be honest at this stage about how planned in your promotional activity has been, or how reactive or ad hoc it's been. Maybe put all your adverts, PR, content etc together to see how it all works as one. Does it seem like a coherent brand or are there vast inconsistencies in your communication?

Taking a few moments to review everything you've done as a whole will give you a clear picture of how you need to move forward. If it's not consistent and there's no real thinking behind it, it can make you look unprofessional. If you're asking for people to trust in you and your brand, having regular, coherent communication sends out a positive message on its own. All you need to do then is add in some well considered content that is aimed perfectly at your audience, and you've already won a few major marketing battles. Doing this will cost you a bit of time, but the potential return on investment could be massive. It's a very worthwhile task to get your 'ducks in a row'.

For Company Q, it was quite difficult analysing the promotion as the company had done so little. They had a website and had been using a website designer, but so few things proactively from a marketing perspective had really been done.

I reviewed Google Analytics and saw that website traffic was very low. But that wasn't surprising as the website had been written in house and it sounded highly technical. It hadn't been given any real marketing consideration. It was just there to tick that box.

This didn't mean that I left out the Promotional part of the 4Ps, though. It was just as relevant to detail the lack of marketing promotion as it was to review the little that had been done i.e. the website and a couple of brochures.

As well as considering what has been done,

looking at why things have been done is just as useful. For Company Q, when I asked about the website and brochures, I found that everyone in house really liked what had been produced. The materials spoke in the language of the product development team and therefore had been deemed to be good representations of the company and the products it sold.

However, I only had to look at the poor website traffic, the lack of brochure downloads and the clunky navigation and it told me the items really weren't being received well by customers. But getting the team on board with my more forward thinking ideas was going to be difficult. If you can't see there's a problem then it's hard to believe it needs fixing. I didn't want it to seem that I was just coming in and putting my stamp on things. A true marketer looks at how they can optimise everything they have to best engage with their audience and impact sales positively. That's all I wanted to do. But I knew I had to tread carefully to demonstrate how the changes I wanted to make were going to improve the customer experience and therefore, hopefully, sales. This wasn't personal.

The 4Ps isn't about just listing down things you've done. It's about fully evaluating the current position of a business and finding, through that objective analysis, where you can improve things to gain more success. For Company Q, the Promotion element showed me that I needed to move them away from their existing technical approach and introduce some emotion into the mix. Promotion isn't just about tasks. It's about how those tasks are executed and what the overall perception is. Sometimes just adjusting the focus or slightly amending the words you use can massively affect how your audience interacts with you. For Company Q, I saw quite clearly that's what I needed to do.

Audit Analysis

After you've listed all your facts across the Industry Research, Customer Analysis, Competitor Analysis and the 4Ps, the next step is to evaluate everything. This is the bridge between being objective and turning your data into actions.

If you've put in enough detail then the trends, gaps, positives and issues should become clear. Be as critical as you can. I find it really useful at this point to translate the Audit into a SWOT. This helps you highlight the strengths, weaknesses, opportunities and threats.

I always go through all of the Audit and mark whether the point I've made is a strength or weakness (these are internal elements) or an opportunity or a threat (external elements). It should give you a nice summary then that you can scan over. I find it much easier as a way to digest everything.

But whatever way you choose to do it, this is the part when you start to jot down the key things that need tackling and your ideas of what needs to be included in the plan. You need to dig out where the big issues are and what quick fixes you could make. You still haven't got to the tactics yet, but it's the time to start turning the facts into more proactive thoughts.

Don't spend ages on this. It's just a small task to summarise areas of the Audit and find those trends. It's about gathering your thoughts to help you easily transition to the next step.

The next step is to create the Marketing Strategy.

Marketing Strategy

A Strategy Isn't a Plan

I've come across many businesses where they haven't been able to decipher the difference between a strategy and a plan. Quite simply, a strategy is what you're going to do and the plan is how you're going to do it.

Think of the strategy as laying the foundation. I always say marketing is like building a house. If you go straight in for the roof or windows, they're just going to fall down. You need a strong foundation and then you need to build it up section by section if you want it to be robust and hold.

So your Marketing Strategy gives you those firm foundations and the Marketing Plan deals with the individual elements, or the marketing tactics as they are often known, such as blogging, social media posting and sending out press releases.

If you went straight in and just looked at the tactics, you might decide you're going to blog and do social media, but how will you know what to blog about, or what to post on those social media channels? Or even what social media platforms to use? Without a strategy driving your tactics, it all becomes meaningless actions that you end up doing for the sake of it. Marketing becomes a tick box exercise.

Some of the worst advice I've ever heard given is that all businesses should be on every social media platform. Without knowing anything about the sector, the brand or the type of business, I've heard this advice be given out as if it's fundamental to marketing success. It cuts through all of the research, all of the thinking, all of the strategy and goes straight to the very final aspect: the tactics. It's like getting eleven people together and then telling them to go play football, without any idea of who is playing in what position, who they're playing against or even where they're playing.

So you could do that, yes. You could be on every social media platform. You could argue there's no harm in being everywhere and capturing every lead possible. But actually there could be harm. For starters, it's a lot of work. Then you'll inevitably end up on platforms that don't reach your customers making all that work a complete waste of time. And even if you happen to be the rare business that sells to users across every platform, the ad hoc approach will no doubt end up being irritable noise that puts your potential customers off anyway.

Social media is a place where people go to read up on things, share news, learn, catch up with friends or connect with businesses. Whatever the purpose, people are doing it to meet their own needs. No one goes on social media wanting to be sold to. Therefore, the only way to be successful on social media is to interact as part of the purpose. That is, be sociable. Don't just broadcast messages.

If you aren't playing your part properly, all you do is disrupt the feed. And not in a good way. If someone is scrolling through and your blatant attempts at selling or your meaningless, poorly thought through content pops up in front of them, they may get annoyed. You're not offering them anything, yet you're popping up five times a day and getting in the way of what they really want to look at.

Whatever you do in marketing, the more you can blend naturally into your customers' worlds, the more chance you'll have of success. The less you sell, the more you'll sell. And the only way you can really achieve that is by truly understanding your market and customers (doing the audit) and then carefully building a strategy and subsequent plan that will harness that objective information and turn it into a powerful tool for you.

By jumping straight into the tactics section, you run the risk of not just being ignored, but actually alienating your customers. I've said it before and I'll say it again, if you want your marketing to work, there is no way to cheat the system. Put simply: bad marketing won't just fail, it could be detrimental to your brand.

There is double good news to doing it right, though. Not only will you have a better chance of success by putting in the hard work up front, but by building a strategy and creating a plan, you'll also end up only doing the tactics that you realise will work. You won't be wasting any more time marketing in channels that have no hope of engaging with your audience, or sending out communications that aren't fit for purpose. You'll suddenly have a purpose, a voice and a clear pathway through. You'll actually spend less time marketing, be more efficient and get better results. How good is that!

So now's the time for us to start working on that pathway. Let's get your strategy set up.

A Marketing Strategy is split down into simple elements. I'm recommending that you look at four key areas. These are the decisions you'll make that won't change through the life of the Marketing Plan.

If this is your first ever plan, then I'd suggest making it six or twelve months long. As you get more confident, you might want to make it longer. But for a small business, a short plan is probably wise at first, as you grow.

For the length of the Marketing Plan, be it six or twelve months or whatever you choose, you should firmly stick to all the decisions you make in your strategy. Even if you think it's not working, consistency is vital. If you keep chopping and changing, firstly it renders your whole plan null and void and this entire exercise becomes a waste of time. Secondly, you won't be able to see any trends that you can then use in the future, as you'll have inconsistent data. And finally, even if you doubt your decisions three months in, having a consistent message that is well thought through can only be a positive. It conveys that you're steadfast and reliable and you're not changing your mind all the time.

Unless the decisions you made are having an adverse effect e.g. you didn't realise that your message was offensive or you totally overlooked a certain segment, then stick to what you decide upon. Have faith in the process. Marketing is a long term game and you will see the results.

The elements that I recommend you look at are:

- Marketing Objectives
- Positioning/Message
- Segmentation
- Targeting

That's it. Four simple areas that will give you a strong direction and a firm foundation. Pull these together and your marketing will automatically become more professional and more streamlined. That alone will provide results.

Let's take a look at these areas in a bit more depth.

1. Marketing Objectives

Marketing Objectives are targets that work alongside the main overall objective. So if you think about the first idea you had as the problem you want to solve, these are the smaller objectives you need to meet to make that possible. The idea is that if you meet all of these, which you can measure to keep a track of, then you should automatically solve your problem.

Marketing Objectives should be SMART objectives. That is:

- Specific – don't be vague, be very clear
- Measurable – you should be able to measure the outcome
- Achievable – you need to actually be able to achieve them. Don't be too ambitious
- Relevant – they have to actually help towards your overall goal(s)
- Time bound – they should be achievable within a certain time frame

As an example, if the problem you wanted to solve or the overall objective was to grow the business, one of your Marketing Objectives could be to get in 100 new leads in the next 12 months, of which 15 convert into sales. That's very specific, it's easy to measure, it's relevant to the overall goal, it's definitely achievable and there is a time limit in which you expect to do it.

Two or three Marketing Objectives here will give you a good scope and will help you when it comes to planning. For example, if you know you need leads in the business, the Marketing Plan can be very heavily swayed towards lead generation activities.

Whatever the Marketing Objectives, they must actually relate to the existing problem you want to solve and you must use the information you found in the audit to guide them. Plucking ideas out of the air will unlikely provide any real results. Keeping everything focused and fact driven is the true pathway to success.

For Company Q, based on the problems that I needed to solve, I decided to write a three year marketing plan. Branding is a long game. It takes a long time to get noticed properly and for that brand identity to stick. Therefore I thought three years would be wise if we were going to reach the goals.

As I said before, if this is your first Marketing Plan then maybe it might be easier to stick to something like six months and see how it goes. But as Company Q had quite big goals in mind, I decided that three years was probably going to be needed to ensure we attained them.

Looking at what we needed to achieve, I chose three key Marketing Objectives:

• The first objective was turnover based, with the targets being incrementally raised year on year. The biggest spike in growth I put for year two, when the bulk of the work would really start to kick in. So it was something like this (please note these aren't the exact figures, this is just a representation of what it looked like):

o Year 1 – £1.5 million turnover
o Year 2 – £3 million turnover
o Year 3 - £3.5 million turnover

• Secondly, I put in a customer retention objective: Company Q had to retain 95% of its customer base every year. This meant that there wouldn't just be a focus on new business, but the marketing would also look at the value of loyal customers

• The final objective looked across the supply chain and how we could build this. Whilst much of the business had been coming in from direct sales, this was also because direct sales were easy to manage. It was all done in house. Therefore the Marketing Plan needed to help improve business elsewhere, and so I put that 10% of business needed to come from distribution by the end of year 1, 15% by the end of year 2 and 20% by the end of year 3

When you have your key objectives in place, you should have much more clarity about what you need to do. But we're not ready to start writing the plan just yet. Next we need to look at your positioning and message.

2. Positioning/Message

Every single well developed brand in the world has a 'position'. Think of it as your marker in the sand of what you stand for and who you are. It summarises your differentiation and will tell your audience why they should buy from you. A position in itself can be an internalised message and then I advise you to translate that into a marketing message that you send out into the world.

Before you even start to think about this, though, the key thing to remember here is that if you want this to work, you need to stick to it. There is no point devising a position and message and then changing your mind a few months down the line because you think it's not working. Remember how I wrote a three year plan for Company Q? That's because branding takes time. Consistency will give you a much better outlook and sticking to something will convey a much stronger message in itself. So whatever your message, stick to it for at least twelve months. Then if you haven't noticed any traction at all in that time (which is highly unlikely if you've created it properly), use the data you will have gathered to find out why and make the necessary changes. At least now your decisions will be more informed.

The best way to devise your position is to use the information from the Marketing Audit. What were the key findings? What is happening in the industry and what do your customers care about? What are your competitors doing and how can you or should you differentiate? What are the key products you sell and what value do you actually offer? What promotions have and haven't worked to date?

Look at absolutely everything and start to jot down the main points and trends that appear.

The only right answer here is that you put something together that will work for you and your customers. This may seem like a very broad scope, but if you use the data in your audit properly then the answer should be easy to decipher.

For Company Q, alongside the findings that we were the only company to offer a bespoke solution, our products were also of high quality. There were a lot of cheaper products appearing in the market and more and more people were competing on price. We were too expensive to ever compete on price, but we offered a hell of a lot more. Not only did our products have a longer life span because they were better made, but we also offered technical support, meaning that customers were never left on their own should something go wrong. We actually really cared about having a good quality end solution. All of this, in turn, meant we provided a greater overall return on investment than our competitors. Therefore I positioned the company as the only complete solution providers.

The marketing wouldn't be product focused but solution focused, with the support added into the mix. Something other people just weren't providing. This gave us our point of differentiation and the general message that we should be sending out to the market.

When you know what your position is, the next step is to create the words of the marketing message that you'll consistently send out to the market. It could be a strapline, for example, or a tagline on your direct mails and advertising. This is where you need to take the analytics and blend them with your creative juices. How can you make your position and your brand sound appealing, and how will that message aid you in reaching your Marketing Objectives?

Let's look at some very famous examples.

Tesco - Every Little Helps
This strapline has been around for a long time, and it's easy to see why. It really works. Tesco is middle of the road in terms of its customer base and is – at the time of writing - the top performing supermarket. "Every Little Helps" supports the brand completely. Whether it's talking about the savings that people can make across the store each time they shop, or the incremental rewards they can get via the Clubcard loyalty scheme, Tesco is all about the little things that make a difference.

The slogan also touches on a very old saying so it can't possibly be misunderstood by its audience. Simplicity works, but when you combine that with the actual depth of what Tesco has done, you've struck gold. No wonder they haven't changed it in twenty years.

L'Oreal - Because You're Worth It
This slogan actually first appeared in 1973 and was "Because I'm Worth It" back then. According to L'Oreal's own website, its goal is to "offer each and every person around the world the best of beauty in terms of quality, efficacy, safety, sincerity and responsibility to satisfy all beauty needs and desires in their infinite diversity." It's all about giving people the right to make their own decisions and

doing this with a strong code of ethics. Back in 1973, it spoke directly to women during the rise of feminism, and today it speaks just as loudly to a more diverse range of people. It's clever, resonates with its audience and fits in with L'Oreal's position in the market. That's what every brand should strive for.

Apple: Think Different

Apple has never been shy about its values. From the outset, it was all about innovation and making things better for its customers. And this isn't just what they talk about. It's ingrained in everything they do. There are three core elements to Apple's brand position: simplicity, creativity and humanity. Through its clear strategy, Apple has been able to revolutionise the industry, and the company has obtained incredible customer loyalty. This is a prime example of how consistency pays off. Think Different sums up everything they do, and it also acts as a message to its audience, asking them to think in a different way too. It's simple, clever, speaks to its audience and works alongside the brand positioning perfectly.

Caffè Nero: The Italian Coffee Co.

Caffè Nero had a set idea from day one. In the company's own words, "Founder Gerry Ford, armed with a passion for coffee, had a vision to create traditional Italian cafés across Europe; places that would serve very high quality coffee and serve as neighbourhood meeting spots." These two elements are at the core of the brand: high quality coffee with a neighbourhood feel.

The company always keeps to its roots, taking one step at a time. There aren't ambitions to suddenly take over the world. They also keep their coffee reasonably priced, choose their food ranges carefully and strive for a European feel. There is no other coffee shop like it and sticking to this brand position is what will give Caffè Nero continued success.

When it comes to creating your own message, think carefully about how you want your business to be perceived. You need this message to last for the long haul and you need to feel proud of it. All of the examples work because they represent the company perfectly and they resonate with the respective audience. That's what you need to keep in mind.

3.   Segmentation

Segmentation is the section of the strategy that decides who you're going to market to. It breaks down your audience. This is where you need to go back to your audit and look at your Customer Analysis. You should have listed every possible group of people or business types that you can sell to, and you should have analysed them. That's the hard work done. Now you have to decide, out of them all, who you should market to. Choosing two or three segments is enough. If you only focus on one then you're limiting yourself, but by doing too many, your resources will be pulled very thin and you may end up diluting your message.

There is no right or wrong here. It has to come down to what you believe is best based on the data you pulled together in the audit and what goals you want to achieve. Sometimes having a mixture of buyers and influencers could be good. But influencers are a much longer game, so you also need to think about what your objectives are.

All the decisions you make here should be directly built upon the original problem you wanted to solve, the Marketing Objectives and your research. This means that the answer is often obvious.

For Company Q, there were ten different business types that I identified in the Customer Analysis and I actually chose six segments to focus on. But remember, this was over a three year plan, and some of them could be easily grouped together. There was only one influencer in the group, the rest were all active purchasers, and individually they would all directly contribute to meeting the Marketing Objectives. This was a complex approach, but the objectives were big. It was very possible to meet all of them, but it required some clever thinking.

Not all plans need to be this ambitious. The only thing that matters is that they work to meet the goals and they work to the resource available. My only job was to execute this plan. It meant it could be a bit more complicated as there was the resource to make it happen. If you're an SME running your own marketing, or with limited extra help, then the plan needs to work to that resource. If you can only spare half an hour a day, how can you maximise that time? Or if you do decide to spend more time on it or get in some extra help, what is the return on investment?

If you do ramp up your marketing, do it in a way that is actually going to work. More time doesn't necessarily mean adding in more social media posts. It could mean you'll market to two distinct segments, in which case you'll need two different marketing tacks. If we go back to the toy shop example, then the two segments could be children aged between 5 and 12 and then adult enthusiasts. You'd never market to them in the same way with the same message. They're completely distinct and this would take up more resource to get right. But the return on investment could be huge, making it a very worthwhile decision.

It all comes down to what's manageable and what's right. Don't be too ambitious, but don't be so narrow you shoot yourself in the foot either. Look at the data you have and be honest.

When you've chosen your segments, you then need to make sure that an ongoing action is to know them. And I mean properly know them. The more you can learn about and understand the customers you're marketing to, the better response you'll get from them. Whether you do that as part of the planning stage, or whether you build it in as an action for the plan, such as sending out polls or surveys, that's totally up to you. It comes down to what information you gathered in the audit and how much time you have. Whichever way you decide to do it, though, don't underestimate the power of building customer personas. Knowing each of your segments inside and out is a must.

4.   Targeting

The final element to the strategy is targeting. You've chosen who you're going to sell to, so the next thing to do is decide what you're going to sell to them.

Let's go back to the toy shop example. I suggested that two of the segments could be children aged between 5 and 12, and then adult enthusiasts. When it comes to targeting, for the children you might decide to focus on toy cars, dolls or action figures. It could be individual products or whole product ranges. It depends on what you think is best. For the adult enthusiasts, it could be board games or model kits.

All you need to do at this point is decide on the products or services for each segment. That's it. It's not about making ground breaking decisions. It's about giving you a solid foundation so that your marketing activities have clarity and focus.

For Company Q, I might have chosen six segments, but we had a very limited product range, so that meant I would be targeting distinct segments with the same product. This then gave me a much easier job. The brand position and message would always be the same, and there were just two product ranges that I was targeting the segments with. This meant the only thing I needed to worry about was tweaking the more specific marketing elements when it came to speaking to the different segments. But that's what I'd decide upon in the plan. From a strategic point of view, things were very clear.

When you've pulled together your Marketing Strategy, you too should have given yourself a very firm foundation. You now know exactly what you need to achieve. You know what the brand position is and what your overarching message is. You also know exactly who you're selling to and what you're targeting them with. Suddenly the broad scope of marketing is much smaller and much easier to deal with.

So now you know what you're going to do. The final stage is to look at how you're going to do it. This is the point where you can get a bit more creative.

Marketing Plan

This is the section where you decide what marketing activity you're going to execute to meet your Marketing Objectives.

If your plan is going to work then you need to make sure that every decision you make works alongside the Marketing Strategy. If it doesn't somehow directly aid meeting your Marketing Objectives, doesn't complement the brand, isn't aimed at your segments, and doesn't promote the target products or services, then don't do it. And this is a very good thing. It makes all of your decisions much easier.

In marketing, it's just as important that you make the decisions on what you're not going to do as it is to choose what you are going to do. If you like the sound of an activity or your competitors are all doing it, yet you can't see how it fits in with your strategy, then don't do it. Just because other people do it, doesn't mean it will work. Just because it looks interesting or you feel passionately about doing it, doesn't mean it will work. Selecting tactics that are aligned with your strategy is the only way to give you the best possible chance of success. In business, that's all that matters. Be wise and sensible, and utilise the hard work you've already put in.

Nine Areas of the Marketing Mix

Whenever I write a plan, I always break down the activity into nine areas. These aren't distinct areas. They will all overlap at some point. But what it always ensures is that I never overlook an activity. There might not be any relevant activity in one of the areas, but it's better to say there's nothing we can do here than forget about something that you later realise could have been important. Therefore, I encourage you to take some time to think about each of these areas and write down all the relevant actions that you could execute within each one. But again, it's just as valid to say there's nothing relevant here as it is to list twenty points. Just be truthful to your strategy and what you're trying to achieve.

Here are the nine areas I work to:

- Branding
- Digital
- PR & Advertising
- Literature
- Data
- Customer Acquisition
- Customer Retention
- Events
- Internal Communications

Let's take a deeper look at each element.

1. Branding

This is where you touch upon all of the elements that relate to your brand and general brand awareness. It's quite a broad area, but it has always helped me think about the little extra things that I might have otherwise overlooked.

At the obvious end, do you need a logo? Do you have a colour palette? Do you need to develop brand guidelines? Brand guidelines are useful if other people, such as Marketing Consultants or Agencies, are working with your brand and you need everyone to understand what your brand is, what it looks like, how the logo is to be used and what the tone of voice must be like.

Also in this area you can look at such things as do you need branded pens, a pop up banner or business cards? Would it be useful to have items produced that are simply there to promote your brand?

You might also want to consider email footers, letter heads and compliment slips, or any other materials that will showcase your logo. Even if you have all that in place, it might be worth updating some items or checking that everything is consistent. This is the area to consider all these sorts of things.

For Company Q, although there was a brand, no one had ever been a brand champion before, so the plan needed to make sure that I adopted that role. I created some brand guidelines and educated everyone on the importance of consistency. Everything from compliment slips to email footers were updated, ensuring that everything across the company was aligned. It made us look far more professional.

If you only ever think about marketing promotion, you miss all of these small but fundamental tasks. Marketing is about far more than lead generation.

2. Digital
This section covers everything within the online world. This is the biggest area on the list, so let's take it step by step.

Websites
Firstly, do you have a website? If no, then simply to get a website might be a task here. If you do have one, then you should review it alongside your strategy. Does it mirror your new position and does it properly convey your brand message? If not, then that's a definite task to add to the list.

You might want to consider things such as how does your website speak to your chosen segments? Are the target products or services clearly promoted? It might be that you need to add in a couple of landing pages or a few extra pages to better highlight the key areas that you've identified in your strategy.

In this section it's also worth going back to the Promotion area of the 4Ps in your audit. Did you notice anything that needed amending or updating on your website? If you examined your Google Analytics, were there any obvious weaknesses? Is no one reading your blogs or is no one visiting a specific product page? This is the time to list what you're going to do to counteract any issues you've found.

It may be that you decide you want to start a blog as that will work well to reach your chosen segment(s). If you're targeting more than one segment, you can still have just one blog, but you could use categories to let the audience know what the blog relates to. So if it's a more technical blog, you could categorise it as technical or know-how. If it's about an industry trend, categorise it as that. You can even categorise your blogs by vertical markets, if that will work well for your chosen segments. This means you don't have to have completely separate areas for different audiences. You are one brand, after all. You just need to make sure that your audience can find everything they need to with ease.

As with anything in marketing, start with the end in mind. Think about what you want to achieve and then decide how best to achieve it working within your own resources. For example, you might love the idea of having a blog, but if it takes a long time to write it and renders very little in the way of results, there is no viable return on investment. Only write a blog if you think it will somehow help you reach your Marketing Objectives.

For Company Q, the audit noted that the existing website was far too technical and hadn't been written with any particular audience in mind. Therefore I decided the best thing to do was start again. A proper scope was needed, specifying exactly what was to go on the website and how it was to develop. By starting all over again, we could get a website that properly supported the business and would be more user friendly for customers.

Social Media

This is one of the most talked about areas of modern day marketing. That's a good thing and a bad thing. Good in that there are loads of opportunities and it can be a free tool. Bad in that everyone else is marketing on social media and so it's hard to stand out.

Unless you absolutely know that your target market isn't on social media, then it's always good to have some presence. But be honest about how much you're really going to sell on there and how much it will be for brand awareness. If you're going to focus on the latter more, then again you need to think about how much time is wise to spend posting. It isn't a one size fits all approach.

The next step is to think about the platforms you're going to use. The only answer here is to look at your chosen segments and be honest about where you think they spend their time. You can take a look at something like Sprout Social to help you decide what to use as it will give you more details on the demographics of each platform.

If your chosen segment doesn't typically use the platform then you have to ask yourself why you'd market on it. Adding posts takes time, and if you're never reaching your audience then it offers absolutely zero return on investment. It makes bad business sense.

I meet a lot of businesses who constantly market across multiple platforms without any understanding as to why, and they often render very little results, if any at all. You need to be strategic in what you do if you want to get anything out of the task. It won't work any other way.

Having chosen your segments, you should be able to easily identify the most relevant platforms to be on. Then the next step is content.

I would highly recommend that you create a content plan. Three to six months in the first instance is probably enough. This may seem like a big task, but now you've got your strategy in place, it's not a blank canvas. You have target products or services that you decided upon in your strategy, so for starters your content plan needs to push these.

A bit of outright selling isn't a bad thing.

However, generally on social media, the less you sell the more you'll sell. You need to keep the content social if you want the best chance of engagement. Don't broadcast but start a conversation. Ask questions, start polls, share your blogs, offer discounts or product promotions, offer insight into the company, share best practice, provide advice, make people laugh, showcase your case studies or testimonials, post your videos and entertain your audience. There is so much you can do, but it needs to work in line with your strategy. That means it needs to help you achieve your Marketing Objectives.

Your content plan could have, say, two posts a week over a twelve week period. That means you need to think of just twenty-four things to say. If you spread it over a mix of blogs, articles, case studies, questions, general company news, video sharing and the odd product promotion/discussion, you'll probably think of more than twenty-four. Then all you need to do is like, share and comment on a few other people's posts in between and you'll have a very active, content rich social media presence. And none of it will be ad hoc, last minute posts when you know you haven't posted in a while. Nor will it be too much content that you just end up irritating your audience by constantly dominating their feed.

Make sure you add into your plan to track your analytics on a regular basis so that you know what's working and what isn't, and you'll be in a very good position.

Company Q had no social media presence at all. Looking at the audience and how best to interact with them, I decided to introduce Twitter and LinkedIn pages and then I created a content plan posting just once a week. From the research I did in the audit, I knew we weren't going to get a vast amount of business from social media, so I needed to put in the effort where we were most likely to gain the rewards. However, I knew that not having a presence would be unwise as customers often look up businesses before they buy. Therefore I wanted to post professional, informative content to support the brand, but, as I was the only marketing resource, I needed to think carefully about which channels I could get the most out of based on the limited scope. This proved to be the best decision. Social media is a powerful tool, but it isn't always the answer.

Affiliates

Linking to other websites and associating yourself with other businesses can be very useful. Just the act of getting yourself listed on industry directories can not only get you noticed, but could also help your SEO. It's worth here thinking about what you could do.

For Company Q, I registered the company on every relevant industry directory I could find and linked the listing back to the Company Q website. I just researched directories here and there, adding the company whenever I had time. It wasn't a vital task, so I didn't give it much dedicated resource, but it definitely paid off. I even got other directories asking to list Company Q, and I got offered PR slots and a few other opportunities, meaning a little bit of effort grew exponentially. Whilst this activity didn't bring in loads of leads, it just helped to boost the foundation. I call this a brand explosion. Others call it surround sound marketing. Either way, after about a year of slowly adding Company Q to everywhere I could find, no one in the industry could look without seeing something about Company Q. It got us noticed. I was later told by industry figures that I'd put Company Q "on the map". You can't do this overnight, but gradually building up an online presence that moves beyond your own website or social media is a great way to get people noticing you.

Emails

Whether it's sending out a newsletter, announcements or e-bulletins, emails can be a useful way of directly speaking to customers, either existing or prospective. If you do think this could help you meet your objectives, firstly I'd recommend coming up with a proper content plan so that all of your content is informative and properly considered. Then think about the system you want to use. Don't just send out mass emails from your regular inbox. You could end up getting blacklisted. Use MailChimp or one of the many other email platforms out there.

For Company Q, I decided to send out a newsletter aimed at current customers only. But let's look at this more in the Customer Retention section.

3. PR & Advertising

I've found that PR is often a massively underutilised area of marketing. Sending out news about your company or writing interesting articles can be a very cost effective way to get your name out there.

As an example, if one of your target products was a new release, then make sure you write a press release about the launch of this new product. Don't just put it on social media - spread the news as wide as possible. It's so easy and can be massively effective.

The only thing to make sure you consider here is to keep the news newsworthy. Ask yourself whether anyone else would be interested. If you think they would, go for it. If you're not so sure, perhaps consider a specific angle that could make it more appealing to your audience.

Make sure you definitely also think about case studies and how you can use these as part of your PR. People love to read about or view videos about how things have worked for others. It also helps to create trust in your brand as it's not just taking your word for it. It's sharing a story about someone else.

In addition, consider awards. There are awards for all different business types, whether it's niche industry ceremonies, local area celebrations or large national events. Putting your business forward for an award can be a fantastic PR opportunity, and there are many award entries that cost nothing. If you do pay, again I'd recommend thinking about the return on investment. How relevant are the categories, will you have the time to give the entry form the consideration it needs and what are your chances of getting shortlisted? Even getting shortlisted will get you promotion, but don't go for it just on the off chance. If you're going to do it, put the effort in to give yourself the best possible chance of winning.

For Company Q, PR was a massive part of the budget. The industry still very much read and relied on trade publications for news, so I made sure the company was featured in as many magazines and online news sites as possible. I regularly sent out company updates and product news. As soon as there was anything even remotely interesting to say, I sent it out as a press release. I also worked with the sales and product development teams to help come up with interesting articles about where the industry was going or technical insight. Throughout the three year plan, rarely a month went by when the company wasn't being featured in some way across the press. As part of that brand explosion I talked about previously, the impact was huge. It made Company Q seem much bigger and highly authoritative, and it pushed forward the brand proposition.

It's easier if it's a larger company with lots going on, but even for sole traders, whenever there is news, be it a case study, new business win, a new qualification gained or just some important insight, the more you can do with PR, the more you'll get your brand out there.

Aiming for three or four news stories a year is a great place to start and will make a massive difference.

Next to think about is advertising. This could be online, in magazines, on the television or even radio. There are so many possibilities. Again, the important thing to think about is how it can help your strategy. Where and how you advertise will also depend on whether you're a local business or a national chain, but there are opportunities for both.

If you've got a broad local reach then radio advertising might work. Or if you've got a specific niche with national coverage, then perhaps finding the relevant trade magazines will be the perfect place. You could advertise on their websites to save costs. If you're considering social media advertising, make sure you choose the platforms carefully and really consider your target audience.

It all comes down to your strategy. Advertising is definitely more of a long game. It's highly unlikely you'll post an advert and instantly get a ton of leads. But brand awareness can make a big difference if you use it strategically. Look at what you want to achieve and decide what's best.

As one of the key objectives was to get Company Q known in the market, advertising became vastly important. I needed a simple and effective way to create lots of brand awareness. Therefore advertising was where I spent most of the marketing budget. But I chose where to advertise carefully, and I did a mixture of print and digital advertising to give a fair spread.

In terms of content, there was a combination of general brand awareness adverts and lead generation ones (see more about that in the Customer Acquisition section). This meant that I was not only aiding my first objective, but also supporting the second lead generation objective at the same time. It was a far better use of time and money.

We did get a few leads directly from the adverts, but what we got more of was pure brand awareness. The sales team could attest to it. When I started, Company Q was generally an unknown entity in the market. Two years down the line, everyone in the industry knew who we were. When the sales team introduced themselves, they didn't have to explain the company or the products anymore. We were immediately recognised and this was a massive achievement.

This meant that future sales and marketing

activities would be more readily listened to and appreciated, improving our chance of engagement. Yes, this was a very long game, but by doing it properly, keeping to the strategy, and remaining consistent and focused, the results were huge.

Some people say it's hard to prove a return on investment from advertising. However, I have always disagreed. Return on investment comes from solving your problem, and if advertising helped you to do that, there's an obvious return on investment. If I hadn't have put the budget into advertising, I don't believe we would have seen the brand grow in the market in the way it did in such a relatively short space of time. If you know what you want to achieve, then return on investment becomes much easier to track. It all comes down to working to business objectives. Know what you want and you'll know if you've achieved it or not. That's how, on this occasion, I could demonstrate that the advertising paid off.

4. Literature

For this section, I always advise that people don't think about what brochures could be produced, but think instead about where the gaps are. Today, websites replace the need for a lot of literature, so that's why I say only do what you need to i.e. what the website doesn't cover. This could be more detailed product PDFs that you email to prospective clients. You could even have these as downloadable documents from your website if you think people may want to keep them and review them. But is it worth printing them? Decide how much they'll be used.

If you attend a lot of events, there will likely be a

need to have flyers, leaflets or brochures to give away, or you may decide that direct mail works for you and you need something printed to go with your covering letter.

The only limitations here are on what you think you'll actually use and what will sit on the shelf for years and ultimately just get binned. Think carefully about where the gaps are and only focus on that.

For Company Q, with quite technical products, there was a need to produce and print brochures. They were regularly requested and given away. I also put them on the website to download so that people could keep them and refer to them whenever they wanted.

There was a need here at the time, but I consistently monitored it. I tried to produce as few documents as possible, with brochures having enough information in them that they could have multiple uses.

Think about the gaps and only ever do what is needed. It can be too tempting to think that you need a brochure or flyer, but only do it if you're actually missing not having one.

5. Database

Another often overlooked area is that of marketing data and databases. But with GDPR, it's absolutely vital that you consider it.

The first thing to definitely consider in your marketing plan is where your data is kept. Also, how secure is it and is it GDPR compliant?

If you don't have a database, you might want to look at introducing one. Perhaps you've got a spreadsheet, and that's fine if it's not taking up too much time to manage and use it. Nowadays CRM systems are very cost effective, so if you are struggling, it might definitely be worth exploring a more automated system.

You should also explore how clean your data is. Is it up to date? Perhaps it is all there but it's quite messy and unusable? Could you confidently do a mail merge directly from your database? Does it matter?

List down any and all actions that you need to take to make sure you're not wasting time with a poor system. Simple tasks to correct problems here can save masses of time moving forward, and these most definitely need to be a part of your marketing activity. If your data isn't fit to be used, you may have a problem. If you're not GDPR compliant, you need to sort it out.

Then what about how much data you have? Perhaps one of your actions is that you need to grow your database. You might decide here to add a "subscribe to our mailing list" button on your website. This is where you can see that all the areas aren't distinct, as your digital activity may merge with your database actions. But it's a good exercise to think purely about data and how you can use it as part of your marketing activity.

For Company Q, there was an existing CRM system but it had never been properly scoped out and it wasn't totally fit for purpose. This was mainly because it had never been anyone's specific job to look after it. The data was messy and not fit for marketing activity. I could never have done a mail merge from the data. Therefore, a key task was to properly scope out the system and make it user friendly, and then tidy up all the data. This wasn't an easy task and it took a lot of time up front. However, a few weeks of pain meant that I had years of easily using and maintaining the data afterwards. And a better system also encouraged other members of the business to look after the data as well.

As with anything I've talked about in this book, only ever put the effort in when you know you'll get something positive out of it. I knew I was going to be doing a lot of direct mailing and customer analysis, therefore I needed a system that would support that. If your spreadsheet is working just fine and you're managing everything perfectly, then don't start to add tasks to your list that aren't necessary. Just make sure that your data is protected and you're GDPR compliant.

6. Customer Acquisition

Whilst you might argue that PR, advertising and digital activity might all be about getting new customers, I put this area in to deliberately think more in terms of marketing campaigns or promotions.

If lead generation is one of your objectives, this is where you need to specifically think about how you're going to generate those leads.

You could do a direct mail campaign, an email campaign, a product promotion, a discount based on certain terms, or a short term marketing message designed deliberately to grab attention. Whatever it might be, think about what you can do that will help you meet your Marketing Objectives. If you've added in a lead related SMART objective, you'll know how many leads you need to generate and in what time frame. Now you need to decide exactly how to make that a reality.

You may devise activities that would fall in other

areas, like extra social media posts, a new landing page on your website or extra literature, but at least you haven't overlooked anything.

Focused lead generation activity isn't easy. Sometimes it needs more of a buzz around it. Think about what you can do and how you can maximise success. But don't forget to always keep your chosen segments and targets in mind.

For Company Q, there were two Marketing Objectives that I needed to consider: growing the turnover and increasing sales in the supply chain. Firstly I looked at the products that were sold in house and I did three campaigns – one for each year of the plan.

For year one, it had to be about generally making people aware of the company, but I also promoted our latest product as part of a three tiered direct mail campaign. So whilst I was sharing general news about who Company Q was, there was a more forced product push in the middle of it. With some strong copy and a catchy slogan, we managed to generate three times the amount of leads that were expected, which we were all delighted with.

Whilst this was all going on, the product development team was writing a formal guide that was to go out to the industry offering training on the new product. It was a particularly technical product. It was a leap forward in terms of innovation, but required a very different approach to anything the industry had seen before. We weren't the only ones manufacturing this type of product, but we'd decided it might help to be one of the few to educate the audience on best practice usage.

The decision to produce this guide had been made before I'd started, but as soon as I got wind of it, I knew it could be massive. Therefore, in year two I wrote a marketing campaign plan around it, I turned it into a properly branded up book and we gave it away for free (upon my insistence) behind a data capture form on the website.

We had 300 downloads in the first few months. This was incredible. I then used extracts of the text for blogs, PR and workshops. We took this idea and squeezed the life out of it. That's what you need to do. Get a good piece of content and make it last. Use it everywhere. Get people as excited about it as you are.

We had about 600 downloads of the book by the end of the second year of the plan, and it resulted in more leads than the sales team could handle. This was totally unexpected, so I needed to tweak my plan to make things more manageable. At the start of year three, as a reaction to the incredible results of the marketing, I devised a lead scoring system. It meant that the sales team would know which hot leads to tackle first, thereby leaving the cold leads for when they had the time. These were the leads that were highly unlikely to convert anyway.

The reason the campaigns worked so well was that they were aimed at our segments, they featured a target product, they aligned with our brand and messaging, and then we pushed them out everywhere we could. They were well thought through, gave the audience something of value and mirrored perfectly what the company stood for.

For the final campaign, we once again sent out a direct mailer. For this, I analysed two years of data to come up with a message and ideas that would help the company reach the final objectives. I had found out that whilst the company sold a range of products, most customers were only aware of the products they actually bought and, as a general rule, they tended to know very little about the range as a whole. Therefore, year three became a cross-selling campaign aimed at educating our audience on what else we could do for them.

We were still getting leads in from the year two campaign, and year three's campaign was nowhere near as successful. But it didn't need to be. We just needed something different to take us over the line and meet those targets. And that's exactly what we did.

When it came to growing sales in the supply chain, it was slightly more difficult. The first thing I did was forge better relationships with each distributor. I made sure they had all the necessary information they needed and I offered the new brochures and marketing materials. I couldn't do much more from a specific lead generation point of view, but I knew that the brand explosion work would aid sales here. As the company and products became better known in the industry, sales naturally increased. None of this was as dramatic as the in house sales, but it didn't need to be. I was right to focus my efforts where we could gain the biggest returns.

7. Customer Retention

Customer acquisition is important for any growing business, but customer retention can be just as vital. Securing loyalty from your customers can make a real difference to your long term success. And it costs a lot less to keep current customers than it does to bring on new ones.

So in this section you need to think about how you can increase sales to your existing buyers and encourage customer loyalty. This means thinking about how can you upsell or cross-sell to those who are already buying from you. This isn't easy, but some small bits of low cost activity here focused on your current clients could have a big impact on your long term profit.

If you remember, one of the objectives I made for Company Q was to retain 95% of our current customers year on year. I did this by firstly introducing a customer only newsletter. You couldn't get it if you weren't a customer, and it listed all the important company news. It made them feel more valued and somehow 'in the club'. Secondly, we created a special area of the website just for customers. Behind a login, they could access a whole raft of information to help make their lives easier.

I'd found in the audit that our customers were having to constantly phone up to request certain items, like product specifications or more detailed information. Therefore, I proposed that we made it all available to customers online behind their own personal login. What was more, we could then track very easily what was the most popular information and what was never accessed, so it worked in our favour too. This was a massive project that took a long time to get right, but it helped to secure loyalty with our customers and gave us an edge that no one else had. It also freed up more time for staff as we didn't have as many calls to deal with. If you look at the return on investment, it completely paid off.

Finally, I planned in some corporate hospitality. Our customers would be our guests at industry events and we'd spoil them whenever we could. With the Bribery Act in place, you need to be careful here. But there is plenty of scope to do this right so it's perfectly legal and it works.

What could you do to make sure your customers are better off sticking with you than looking elsewhere? And how would that help you meet your objectives?

8. Events

Next is events. This can cover exhibitions, workshops, seminars, webinars, networking or open days, just as examples. There are loads of options here, and sometimes they can be high budget. But they can also come with great returns. When we meet and interact with people we build better relationships with them.

Obviously, you must think about what works in relation to your strategy. If you do decide that some sort of event will help you reach your goals, before you do anything else, you need to focus on what you can do to get the most out of it. Just turning up at an exhibition or filling a room full of prospective clients for a seminar isn't good enough. You need to make the experience worthwhile for everyone involved. The more you can maximise every minute of the event, the better it will be.

If you're at an exhibition, how can you capture business cards and get people interested? If you're running a seminar, make sure the content is really interesting, you throw in activities and regular breaks, and you have a call to action. Don't let them just walk away. Have a follow up course, more material for them to look at, or give them a free book to digest. Whatever it is, think of what you want to get out of it and then drive everything towards that.

For Company Q, exhibitions were too costly. I knew I could get more out of the budget doing other activities. I explored this carefully and it wasn't an easy decision to make, but considering the small resource, I knew it was for the best.

The main events we held were training courses, which took place in line with the technical books we produced. Having a theme and consistent message running through everything worked brilliantly. It gave us a firmer foundation and people really started to understand who we were and what we were about. Linking different parts of the nine elements together will give you the best chance of your tactics working. These aren't nine separate areas, and, knowing that, I made the events work in line with the Customer Acquisition activity, which worked in line with the website and social media, which worked in line with literature and branding, and so on. You get the picture. Synergy in marketing is so important.

Whatever event you hold, it might end up taking up a good percentage of your budget. So make sure you use the money wisely.

9. Internal Communications

The final area is internal communications. This is again something that not many people think about.

This could be relevant whether you have a team of fifty or you work for yourself. It's all about how you communicate to the people who help you make it happen.

Let's look at the bigger teams first. Once you've

written your marketing plan, make sure you share it with all of those who it will affect. That is everyone who has anything to do with marketing or customers, from credit control to customer service to the sales team. If they don't know what the key messages are and what information is going out about the company, they could very well contradict it. Or they could look very stupid when they don't know about the latest promotion that's running. It's a simple task to keep your colleagues up to date and could be absolutely vital if you want that consistent approach.

If you work by yourself, you still may have a 'team' surrounding you, like your accountant, marketing consultant/agency, a sales person, telemarketer or virtual assistant. Whoever they are, if they have some sort of input into your business, then it can only be beneficial to share your plan with them. If they're on board and understand what you want to achieve, they will aid you in achieving it.

Make sure you share your strategy and plan with anyone who could affect it, and try to get them enthused about what you're trying to achieve. It will make achieving it a lot easier.

For Company Q, I suggested to the directors that they hold quarterly company update meetings where each department could update the whole company on what they were doing. This would allow me to share my big plans with everyone, and I'd also get input from staff during the planning stages. I knew that the more people felt involved in the process, the more they were likely to buy into it.

I also produced a quarterly internal newsletter that allowed everyone across the company to share news. Whereas the formal meetings were run from a management perspective, the internal news could be owned by anyone. I could then put in notes about some of the smaller bits of marketing activity I was doing, always ensuring everyone was in the loop.

As well as this, I sent out monthly marketing reports, sharing stats on website visits, social media followers, press coverage and number of leads gained. It wasn't a mass of information, but it showed that the marketing was being proactive and actually making a difference.

In marketing, we say that other departments are your internal customers, as marketing needs to sell the ideas to colleagues just as much as to those outside of your organisation. If you think of it in this way, then it might help to break down any barriers you come across.

Activity Breakdown

By now you should have a list of all the things you need to do to help you reach your goals. Next you need to be clear about how you're going to manage it.

To give me clarity, I always put all of the activities into a timeline. I do it month by month as that seems easiest.

It should look something like this:

Month 1
- Create pop up banner and order pens
- Begin website updates
- Write social media content plan
- Enter awards
- Write blog content plan

Month 2
- Complete website updates
- Create new product PDF brochure
- Send out product PR
- Send out newsletter
- Social media posting
- Industry directories updating
- Write blog

Month 3
- Begin advertising on trade publication website
- Write blog
- Plan for exhibition
- Create flyer for product promotion
- Social media posting

Month 4
- Send out newsletter
- Continue advertising
- Blog and social media posting
- Work on exhibition
- Write case study

Month 5
- Attend exhibitions
- PR out
- Launch product promotion
- Final month of advertising
- Editorial in trade publication
- Blog and social media posting

Month 6
- Add exhibition leads into database
- Newsletter out

- Blog and social media posting
- Pull together analytics and write next 6 month plan

It can have as few or as many actions as needed, but by doing it like this you'll clearly see what you can manage, and it will help you get a balance of activities month by month.

It also means that you'll no longer have to think too far in the future. Just do the activities each month that you've listed. All the long term thinking is done. Now is the time to execute, which will be far easier because you've got a strategy and a plan.

Targets

The very last section is to list down some targets. These are even smaller chunks that you can measure that will help you keep a track of how things are panning out.

The idea is that if you meet all of your targets, you'll meet your Marketing Objectives, and then you'll reach your overall goal and solve that problem.

These targets need to be very small and easy to track. Try to think of ones across the different areas of the marketing mix and again keep them SMART.

It could look something like this:

Digital
- 500 visits to the website every month by the end of the plan period
- Get 300 Twitter followers by the end of the plan period

PR & Advertising
- Minimum of 10% clickthroughs of any digital advertising banner

Customer Acquisition
- 50 leads directly from the product promotion campaign

Customer Retention
- Minimum 20% open rate of the customer newsletter email

Events
- 100 leads from the exhibition

Keep a track of these regularly, more often than your main Marketing Objectives. If you're way off reaching one of them, that is the time to tweak your marketing activity plan. You can tweak your plan in accordance with these targets as often as needed, just don't alter your strategy.

End Results

For Company Q, the plan worked extremely well. I initially only set out targets for the first twelve months so that I could more easily monitor success and then tweak as I went along. I'd planned that after I saw the year one results, I would set out year two targets, and after that, year three targets. We actually hit all the small targets for year one in the first three months. It was quite unexpected. It seemed that going from nothing to suddenly blasting the industry with a lot of carefully thought through marketing messages made a positive impact. I might have called it a brand explosion, but I was totally in control of where all the shrapnel landed. That control and strategic approach paid off and then some.

In the end we easily hit the Marketing Objectives for year one and two, and only struggled in year three when the impact of something new and different had started to die down. That's when I had to work more with other departments across the company and be even more strategic about what we were going to do.

But overall, my plan achieved everything it set out to do.

None of it was luck, though. The only reason for

the success was good, solid research, followed by a carefully considered strategy and then a wisely selected mix of activities. It definitely helped that everyone bought into the plan, and I worked just as hard on my internal customers as I did on the external ones.

The key lesson here is to focus on making sound decisions and then sticking to them. I stuck to my plan like glue, just making small tweaks as I went along, reacting to industry and company changes, and the new data I was measuring from all of my activities. But whenever I did make a modification to the plan, it was not a knee jerk reaction. And I never budged from the strategy at all.

If you want marketing success, you need to put the work in up front. Just doing lots of stuff and being busy is unlikely to equal success. Doing it with a structured approach will take you far less time overall and will give you far better results. What have you got to lose?

My company's strapline is, "Don't just do marketing, do it right." It couldn't be more important.

Best of luck!

About Lindsay Woodward

After gaining a degree in BA (Hons) Writing & Media, Lindsay knew that she wanted to use her skill set to work in marketing, and straight away got a lucky break temping in a marketing department for a software company in London.

Despite the temporary nature of the role, Lindsay worked hard and made herself indispensable, and was soon offered a contract of employment.

From this initial Marketing Assistant job in 2003, Lindsay quickly moved up the ranks. She gained her first role as a head of department in 2012. This particular company also helped her gain her Professional Diploma in Marketing from the Chartered Institute of Marketing (CIM). Following this qualification, Lindsay was first accepted as a Chartered Marketer, and, at the time this book was published, Lindsay was celebrating her 7th consecutive year as a Chartered professional.

Being Chartered means that Lindsay must stay on top of her professional development and this means regular training, reading and mentoring of others.

In 2018, after a few Marketing Manager roles, Lindsay decided that she could take her skills and experience and help more small businesses tackle their marketing, and she opened up her Marketing Consultancy, Lindsay Woodward Marketing Ltd.

Having always worked for Small to Medium Enterprises, Lindsay has the right knowledge to support SMEs and she fully understands the everyday issues that these businesses face.

Lindsay may have started her career with just copywriting skills, but she has now worked across the full marketing mix and can help with a range of tasks. It's through all of her years working in marketing and her dedication to training and development that has meant she has been able to successfully help many small businesses implement marketing strategies that work and make a real difference.

To find out more about Lindsay Woodward Marketing and the services that are offered, please visit www.l-w-marketing.com.

When Lindsay isn't marketing, she writes novels, but this is her first non-fiction book. If you are interested in finding out more about Lindsay's other books, please visit www.lindsay-woodward.com.